J. H. (Joseph H.) Williamson

G.D. Howe materials

J. H. (Joseph H.) Williamson

G.D. Howe materials

ISBN/EAN: 9783741169793

Manufactured in Europe, USA, Canada, Australia, Japa

Cover: Foto ©Thomas Meinert / pixelio.de

Manufactured and distributed by brebook publishing software
(www.brebook.com)

J. H. (Joseph H.) Williamson

G.D. Howe materials

1889. HOWE'S 1889.

POTATO MANUAL

G. B. HOWE,

SEED POTATO GROWER

NORTH HADLEY, HAMPSHIRE CO., MASS.

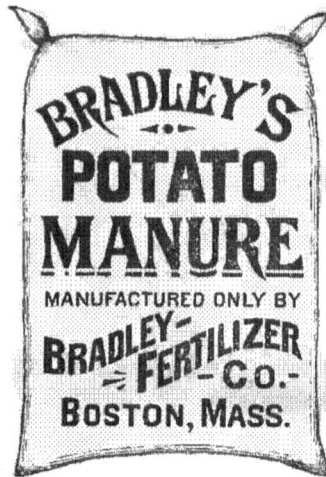

Howe's

Potato Manual

FOR 1889.

EMBRACING MUCH INFORMATION ABOUT THE CULTIVATION OF
THE POTATO AND HOW TO MAKE IT A
PROFITABLE CROP.

TOGETHER WITH

A PRICE-LIST OF OVER 500 VARIETIES OF THIS ESCULENT,

AND

A CLUB LIST OF AGRICULTURAL PAPERS.

BY

G. D. HOWE,

SEED POTATO GROWER,

North Hadley. Mass., Hampshire Co.

AMHERST, MASS. :
J. E. WILLIAMS, BOOK AND JOB PRINTER.
1889.

SOME LEADING AUTHORITIES ON THE MAPES MANURES.

"The Mapes fertilizers, though higher in price than some others, are scientifically, carefully and honestly made. In the use of them we are always pretty sure of good results. We use them every year and have not been disappointed in their action, (May, 1888). They seem to go right to the spot and stay there better than any other sort we have used. We get most excellent results in both corn and potatoes." (Nov., 1888).— *Wilmer Atkinson. Farm Journal.*

"Under average conditions, and in far the greater number of cases, we do not hesitate to name the Mapes Potato Manure as the Best and Most Profitable fertilizer for Potatoes."—*American Agriculturist.*

"The Mapes Potato Manure is certainly as good a fertilizer for the Crops as we can expect to find."—*J. T. Lovett, Orchard and Garden.*

"Its action Approaches Certainty, or as near it as any manure can be expected to do."—*E. S. Carman, Rural New Yorker.*

"Our own experience with various commercial fertilizers has convinced us that with judicious use of the Mapes Manures worn out lands can be Rest red to Fertility Quicker and with less expense, than in any other way."

"The remarkable success which has attended the Mapes fertilizers has given them an enviable reputation and standing, not only in the United States and Provinces, but in Great Britain and other European countries."—*American Agriculturist.*

"Mr. Mapes has studied industriously and has worked conscientiously to help the farmers. I believe he has tried as hard to serve the farmer's true interests as any one in this room. He knows how to make good fertilizers adapted to their needs, and he is making as good ones as he knows how to make. *They are reliable and may be depended upon. You may be sure of getting what you buy— getting what is guaranteed. I am glad to stand here and authoritatively make these statements.*"—PROF. GEORGE H. COOK, DIRECTOR OF THE NEW JERSEY STATE AGRICULTURAL STATION, at a meeting of the State Board of Agriculture, at Trenton, N. J.

The new Mapes Pamphlet (now in press) will contain full details of best and latest methods of growing potatoes, over 500 bushels on one measured acre ; 128 bushels on one-eighth of an acre, and in several cases at rate of over 1000 bushels per acre—truck crops, fruits, etc. Also of **Grand Prize $1000.00,** in gold coin, offered by the *American Agriculturist* and the Mapes Company for the BEST ACRE of Potatoes grown in 1889 and with the Mapes Potato Manure. Mailed gratis. Address

The Mapes Formula and Peruvian Guano Co.,

158 FRONT ST., N. Y.

INTRODUCTORY.

In presenting you with this *manual on potatoes*, the writer wishes at the outset to be distinctly understood. He does not claim to be one of "the lights" on the subject and does not put forth any ideas as authoritative, but rather offers what he says as suggestions for further thought and discussion.

He wishes to be considered a fellow-searcher after new light, as well as a prover of the old, in the art and science of successful potato growing. He has had some experience, has some ideas of his own, has read quite extensively on the subject and gives in this little pamphlet some of the thoughts that have seemed particularly valuable and worthy our consideration.

If the reader finds some new idea here which proves valuable to him, or if he looks at an old familiar fact displayed in a new light, and is therefore better able to appreciate it, or is in some way encouraged to new effort, then both your time and mine will have been profitably spent; but if, on the contrary, you find nothing to cheer, enlighten, or awaken your soul to renewed zeal then our time will have been worse than wasted.

This pamphlet is not put out as a target for critics, though such as have any fault to find with it, or any ideas in it, will receive my thanks for making their grievances known to me before they give the public the benefit of it.

On the other hand, as a little cheer and good will are quite as essential to a man's happiness in life as some more substantial things, it will be the source of some gratification to know whether any are encouraged to take a step in advance, or are set to thinking and experimenting in a direction that will prove profitable or if our business acquaintance proves pleasant and satisfactory.

Wishing you much success, I am, faithfully,

G. D. Howe.

North Hadley, Mass., Jan. 1, 1889.

The Long and Short of It is,

to make two potatoes grow where one grew before, and to get to market with them a week earlier than ever before, and therefore to give each, you and me, two cents where one was before.

A FAMILIAR CHAT.

FERTILIZERS AND OTHER THINGS.

In preparing this little treatise on potatoes the writer is confronted at the outset with the thought that, as the pamphlet is to have a national circulation, he must talk to growers in all parts of the country and so conform to a multitude of circumstances and have something interesting and profitable for each.

It would be very misleading and harmful to lay down any definite method of growing potatoes, or any other crop, for that matter. Consequently it will perhaps be best for us to look over many methods and ideas and see what good we can find in each.

Any farmer to attain success to-day above that of the proverbial "plow-jogger" must be alive, up to the times, ready to meet any new competition, insect enemy, or foe in disease, by a new manifestation of yankee ingenuity (which by the way is not now confined within the walls of old yankeedom) together with the aid of modern science, with a due sprinkling of good old "horse sense," which most successful farmers are credited with possessing.

Every farmer ought to be an experimenter to some extent. With the exception of such farms, which are fast growing scarce, as do not have to be manured in any way, the fertilizer problem is one of the most serious. With probably more than nine-tenths of all extensive potato growers the great question is, how to fertilize with the least money for the greatest returns. Each farmer must answer this question for himself, as probably no one can do it satisfactorily for him.

All sorts of conclusions will be arrived at and all perhaps correct. These would be a few of the results,—nitrate of soda, sulphate of potash, superphosphate of lime, barnyard manure, green crops plowed under, some one of the many special potato fertilizers, or some of the complete commercial fertilizers.

The soils which would afford success with these different fertilizers would be vastly different in their resources and wants, and the different soils and fertilizers could not change places with one another and give any success.

For instance,—the soil that gives a crop with nitrate of soda alone, has a present supply of potash and phosphoric acid and is perhaps

Don't fail to examine carefully every page of this book, as **there is money for you,** in here somewhere.

BUFFALO STANDARD

SCALES

.

MANUFACTURED BY

BUFFALO   SCALE   CO.,

BUFFALO, N. Y.

The superiority of the Buffalo Scales is an established fact. They have been adopted by the U. S. Government, and their reputation is world-wide. These Scales are made of the best materials by the most skillful workmen, and for accuracy, durability and beauty of finish, excel all others.

Every Scale is warranted to give entire satisfaction. Send for Illustrated Catalogue and Price List, to

BUFFALO   SCALE   CO.,

BUFFALO, N. Y.

deficient in nitrogen, which is supplied by the nitrate of soda. The soil which gives good results with sulphate of potash alone has probably been exhausted of its potash and must from some unusual cause have a supply of nitrogen and phosphoric acid. Likewise in the case of the superphosphate, the soil either never had much phosphoric acid in it, or has been cropped with some plant that takes that element in a larger proportion than the two other fertilizing essentials. In the case of the barnyard manure and green crops, the soil, very likely, is of sandy or gravelly nature, devoid of much organic matter and on which the scab can not be induced to come, and may also be poverty stricken in all three essentials, and, of course, when they are supplied to this natural potato soil a good crop is the result.

With the special potato manure or even any good commercial fertilizer made as a general crop manure, the results ought to be satisfactory on a poor soil and even if a little predisposed to grow scabby potatoes under other circumstances.

To illustrate a little farther, to show how a man should use all the light he can get and then be his own guide, a man whose farm is on the fertile meadows, along the banks of the Conn. river, passed, last spring, a farmer who is farther back from the river and on higher ground and whose soil is gravelly, while the latter was planting potatoes. He was putting a small shovelful of barnyard manure in the hill and dropping the potato onto it and covering all at the same time with soil. The passer-by says "Why, is that the way you plant potatoes? I shouldn't get a potato fit to market if I did that way." The potatoes turned out all right, with little or no scab.

As handsome and smooth potatoes as the writer saw at any of the fairs the past Fall, were exhibited at one of our local fairs, and they were grown on hen manure, in a gravelly soil. Again—a certain local farmer says he hasn't had but one decent crop of potatoes during the some several years he has been farming, and that crop was grown on one of the special potato manures; but it cost so much he thought he would see if he couldn't find something else that would do, which was cheaper, but having tried something different each year, he says that the coming season he is going back to that special potato fertilizer again.

Sir J. B. Lawes, of England, wrote, some four years ago, that his

soil had been yielding, for many years, potash enough to grow a crop of potatoes without applying any of that element. With such a soil it is useless to expend money for potash but put it into the other two elements. Of course it is understood that such a process will result in getting to an end of the available potash sometime, the extent of which, however, experiment will only tell. These illustrations are given simply to suggest the idea to some that they can possibly fertilize their land cheaper than they are doing now and attain as good results. It may pay you to do a little experimenting in this direction, by trying several of the single elements or combinations of them to determine whether the soil needs a complete manure or not and if not, what it does need.

Another thing in this connection which some may have to contend with, and we have seen a complaint in this direction during the past season. Where land has a great abundance of lime in it the workings of some special fertilizers are upset by the phosphoric acid of the fertilizer uniting with the lime in the soil, forming a somewhat insoluble compound, which results in the fertilization being as if only nitrogen and phosphoric acid had been applied with the consequent failure of the crop and condemnation of the fertilizer. While the writer wouldn't wish to undertake to say how to best remedy this trouble, he offers as a suggestion that some fertilizer can be found by experiment perhaps, if in no other way, which yields up its phosphoric acid reluctantly and thus the plant will be likely to get more of it than a quick acting fertilizer. Of course barnyard manure is such a fertilizer, but where one don't wish to use this, it is quite probable some substitute can be found.

If barnyard manure must be used, by all means, if it is possible, plow it in, in the fall, which will lessen the evil effects of scab, if potatoes grow scabby on your soil. Perhaps, right here as well as anywhere, we can make a few suggestions on

2

GREATEST SEED OFFER EVER MADE.

——A CHOICE SELECTION OF———

SEEDS

For the Family Garden.

LIST OF SEEDS IN EACH COLLECTION.

Corn Improved Evergreen,	10
Mammoth Iron-Clad Watermelon. The largest, most productive and best melon,	10
Best 6 varieties of Cabbage. A valuable package and one that is sure to please,	5
Best 8 varieties of Tomatoes. A splendid collection of newest varieties,	10
Variegated Pop-Corn. New and handsomest ever seen; ears red white and blue,	15
Nichol's Medium Green Cucumber. (New) Handsome; prolific; a great acquisition!,	10
Improved Guernsey Parsnip. Roots smooth, fine grained, and most excellent quality,	5
Best Varieties of Beets. A splendid selection of finest table sorts.	5

FLOWER SEEDS.

Hollyhock. Grandest varieties, double as roses; all colors in each packet,	10
Portulaca. Handsome hardy annuals; all kinds and colors. A great favorite,	5

In all 10 packets, [besides "extras,"] amounting at regular catalogue rates to   85

Packed with great care and guaranteed to reach their destination in good condition. The above package is put up ESPECIALLY FOR OUR OWN USE by a large New York Seed house. These varieties are grown in immense quantities, and are furnished in large lots at a comparatively small cost, which enables us to *give* a Collection FREE to each new subscriber to the National Farm and Fireside at 50 cents per year. This collection is carefully selected from the best varieties, and guaranteed to please all or money refunded. Five collections and five subscriptions, $2.25. Get up a club at once. This collection cannot be bought for less than 85 cents. No change made as the packets are already put up awaiting your order.

☞Full-sized packets guaranteed.

THE

National Farm and Fireside,

The only agricultural paper at the National Capital

IS NOW IN ITS 15th YEAR AND IS KNOWN AND READ IN EVERY STATE IN THE UNION.

It is a 16 page paper of 64 columns, published twice a month. Subscription price, 50 cts. per year.

Write at once and secure the above described collection of seed FREE. Address,

NATIONAL FARM AND FIRESIDE,
Box 33, Washington, D. C.

SCABBY POTATOES.

Scabby potatoes are the source of considerable annoyance to the farmer, the object of much speculation with the agricultural writer and an unyielding subject of the scientific investigator.

Nothing reliable is known of the cause of this trouble, high authority being about equally divided on it, part believing it to be a fungus growth while others think it the work of wire or other worms.

The Mass. Agricultural Experiment Station has spent four years on the subject and have arrived at only these rather minor results, viz.: That certain soils are very likely to produce scabby potatoes while others almost never do. That scabby or smooth seed has nothing to do with the crop being scabby, as scabby seed was planted on non-scabby soil and produced perfectly smooth tubers while perfectly smooth seed without any hereditary taint of scab was planted in the scab-producing soil and rendered scabby potatoes. That the seed treated with chemicals and compounds usually destructive to fungus growth produces as scabby potatoes as if not treated.

That potatoes grown in the scab-producing soil on a Sulphate, grow less scabby than those grown on any other chemical. This latter conclusion leads to what is now generally acknowledged, that potatoes grown in a soil with scabby proclivities on commercial fertilizers will be by far smoother than if grown on barnyard manure or any fertilizer that has to decompose in the soil about the potatoes.

Whether it be fungus growth, wire worms, chemical action of the soil, atmospheric changes, or something else yet unthought of, that causes the vexatious trouble, it is certain that the commercial fertilizers have a marked effect in lessening and in many cases, entirely preventing it.

With this in view it is advisable to apply some of the fertilizer, say 200 to 400 lbs., according to the make, and the whole amount to be used per acre, in the hill or drill, a part under the seed and a part

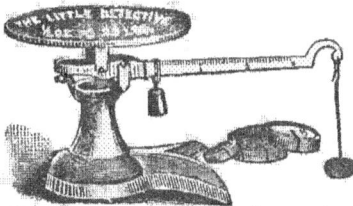

I shall **Give Away** this valuable little scale to my patrons this season. Having it sent, to those who are entitled to it, direct from the factory, so you will get a perfect article and one perfectly new. It weighs from $\frac{1}{2}$ oz. to 25 pounds. See one of my special offers further on which closes the 20th of March. Manufacturer's price is $3.00, at the factory.

IMPROVED FAMILY SEWING MACHINE.

This is the most popular machine made. It is of the Singer Style, manufactured expressly for us, and fully warranted. It contains many valuable improvements, making it the most perfect and useful machine for the price that is made.

The Furniture is Black walnut, Oil Polished, as above represented, with Drop Leaf Table, Five Drawers and Cover Box. With each machine is a full set of attachments, including Rufflers, set of Hemmers, Tucker, Foot Hemmer or Friller, package of Needles, six Bobbins, Screw Driver, Oil Can, extra Check Spring, extra Throat Plate, Gage Screw, Wrench and Instruction Book.

PRICE, $18.

THE HIGH ARM "JEWEL" MACHINE.

PRICE, $22.

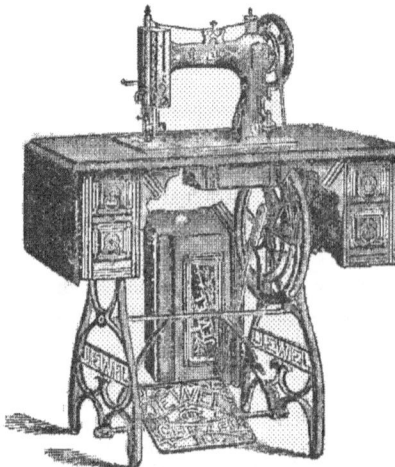

This is the latest improvement in Sewing Machines, and combines all the BEST qualities of high-priced machines, while it contains others, making it superior to any. Its simplicity is a marvel. It contains but little more than half the number of parts of any Lock-stitch or Shuttle Machine. Its new UPPER FEED is very effective, and no change of tension is required from thin to thick goods, which may be turned to any angle, without raising the pressure foot. It has the newest perfect Self-Setting Needle in use, which may be set in the dark. The improved LOOSE WHEEL works automatically, so there is no necessity of turning screws, loosening springs or catches. This machine makes the nicest stitch of any machine without exceptions. Both sides are so even and regular it is almost impossible to tell the right from the wrong side of a seam.

The ATTACHMENTS which are furnished with each machine FREE, are unsurpassed in workmanship, finish or the fine work they will do. The Instruction Book contains a large engraving of each, with full direction for using. The furniture is black-walnut, of the style represented above, and very finely finished. In fact we claim the "Jewel" to be the best made, and to do better work and a wider range of work than any machine in the market. Catalogue of 1000 articles sold at lowest prices sent on application.

CHICAGO SCALE CO., Chicago, Ill.

above it, being careful to let none come in contact with the seed, an inch or two of soil separating them.

While this double distribution of fertilizer in the hill or drill is not very commonly practiced, yet we believe it to be advantageous to do it for the reason that roots will grow towards plant food and as it is natural for them to grow downward they will get hold of the fertilizer under the seed first and early make for the deep moist soil which is a great safe-guard against the evil effects of drought; then as all potatoes are formed above the seed piece, the fertilizer deposited there is ready to do service in keeping off worms and fungus and at the same time help on the growth of the crop. Those who do not already know it will find that the soil least likely to produce scabby potatoes is the sandy or gravelly, or sandy loam, while that most likely to is the heavy loam with an abundance of vegetable mould in it.

Leaving the matter of fertilizers for a little, to speak of them again, we wish to notice the different

METHODS OF PLANTING AND CUTTING SEED.

Probably the most common method of planting potatoes is, after the soil is prepared, to furrow out to the depth of from three to five inches with a small plow, distribute fertilizer in the row, and cover, or drop the fertilizer in the hill, and then the seed, perhaps whole and perhaps cut, along the furrow and cover either with a ridger, plow or hoe With the recent introduction of potato planters which go into a field that is prepared, carrying seed potatoes and fertilizer, and needing only to be guided back and forth to complete the job, a pair of horses and ordinary driver can now do the work of many men, and in most cases probably, more satisfactorily. With this

I shall **give away** until March 20, the following excellent publications : *Herds and Flocks*, of Chicago, subscription price $1.00 per year, a 16 pp. semi-monthly, printed on extra paper and well gotten up. *The Western World, Illustrated*, of Chicago, a large quarterly, finely illustrated, printed on very nice paper and in every way a very presentable journal, subscription price 25c. A publication we shall not be ashamed to give you.

The Western World, Guide and Hand Book, of useful information, cost 50c., 96 pages, cloth bound, colored maps of every state. A little encyclopædia in itself.

See one of my special offers to find how you can get one or more of these publications without cost.

advance in farm machinery, extensive growers, or small ones for that matter, will find a real saving in the first cost of a potato crop.

Then with the potato planters, there are the sulkey cultivators and the sprinkling carts for distributing paris green or other poison over several rows at once, and finally and not the least valuable, the really successful potato-digger.

Speaking of diggers,—probably most who read this will say they are a failure—so they are, all but one or two out of the hundred or more different kinds. We will notice these again when we come to the harvesting of the crop.

Of the methods of planting, one has been watched with considerable interest during the past season and that is known as the Rural New Yorker Trench system. By this method of preparing the soil and planting Mr. E. S. Carman, the editor of the Rural New Yorker undertook to grow over 700 bushels per acre, on an agreement with the editor of the Farm Journal of Philadelphia, that if he succeeded the latter, Mr. Wilmer Atkinson, was to pay $50 to some charity and if he failed he would make this payment.

Mr. Carman paid the money but at the same time demonstrated that the *trench system* had merit in it. The cause of the failure of the crop to exceed 700 bu. per acre was pronounced by the judges to be caused by the ravages of the flea-beetle instead of any lack of merit in the system.

The essentials of the system are, to trench out the soil to a depth of eight inches and a foot wide, distribute fertilizer in the bottom which is stirred into the soil, cover with two inches of dirt, plant the seed, one foot apart in the row, cut so that each piece will have three strong eyes, and cover with soil so that the ground will be level.

The advantages claimed for this system of planting are, the protection of the crop against drought, the rendering of the plant food more available, and the protection of the tubers from sunburn.

A VALUABLE INVENTION.

The Boice Permutation Door Lock.

A COMBINATION Door Lock for the front doors of Residences, Churches, Stores, Banks, Offices, Schools, etc. Any child can operate it. SAFE, SECURE, RELIABLE. No key nor keyhole; cannot be picked; is locked from outside by pressing in a button and simply shutting the door; can be unlocked with gloved hand and in less time than any key lock. A perfect anti-friction lock. Any common spindle with 3 4 inch shank knob can be used. Knobs and spindles furnished to all desiring them, at reasonable prices. No breakage by slamming. No wearing of the parts. The combination can be changed as often as desired. Full directions accompany each lock.

A PERFECT SPRING CATCH,
    A PERFECT NIGHT LOCK,
        A PERFECT DEAD LOCK,
            and THE MOST PERFECT LOCK MADE.

This lock has been patented only about a year and is just being introduced As yet the manufacturers are making only one size and that a large brass lock for heavy doors, but intend soon to have a large variety of styles that will adapt this principle to almost every use a lock can be put to.

See pages 18 and 20 for further details.

While we read recently the adverse opinion of an extensive grower on this method as tried by him, we believe there is real merit in it and that if it can be adopted in some practical way so that the horse and usual machidery can be used, that it will be a decided advance in the cultivation of the crop for profit.

We think the system certainly deserves a wide and thorough test by practical growers. Let us hear what the result is in the fall. Plow out a generous furrow in the field and strew the fertilizer, and then with whatever tool you have mix it thoroughly with the soil, use a subsoil plow if you can't find anything else, letting it into the bottom of the furrow but an inch or two, drop the potatoes and cover with any tool you have that will do the job; in my vicinity people use tobacco ridgers. While covering I should want to try a few rows with the seed covered only two or three inches instead of six as Mr. Carman proposes. It seems as if they would come up quicker and the cultivating would throw the soil into the furrow and cover up the small weeds, thus saving hoeing and still leave the field in level cultivation. Thus perhaps this new and interesting system of planting is sufficiently described to mention some of the common methods. Some farmers mark their ground both ways three or more feet apart and plant at the corners, thus being able to cultivate both ways saving much hand hoeing. This makes considerable more ground to go over in sprinkling poison and gathering the crop. We think however that since the advent of the Colorado beetle that growers have taken to planting thicker, which necessitates richer soil to secure good marketable potatoes. The systems of planting in hills and drills each have their advocates and are too well known to need comment here. Those who have planted in drills may have experienced a difficulty in dropping the seed by its bounding around in the furrow, thus making very crooked rows to bother in cultivating and leaving the hills very irregularly spaced. We saw last summer at the excellent farm of Geo. B. McClellan, of Whately, Mass., a neat and very simple device of his own for obviating this very difficulty. His was simply a square spout made of common narrow boards, leaving a hole in the center 2 1-2 or 3 inches square. This spout was about 33 inches high, had a handle projecting at right angles to one of its sides about six inches from the top, and a tail piece of strap iron nailed to the bottom pointing in the same direction as the handle and about two feet long, bent up at the end to be just 18 inches long from the center of the spout, the dis-

All **Special Offers** and Premiums on **Potatoes** are at an end after March 20, when orders can be received only at catalogue rates.

3

All who are interested in this lock are invited to send in their names for special circular of it. The requests will be put on file and as soon as the circulars are out copies will be sent them, which will be some months yet, as the company have just begun the manufacture of the locks. Any who think they would like one or more of these perfect locks without waiting for the special circular to come out, can write to that effect and their inquiries will have prompt attention.

☞ *See pages 16 and 20 for further details.* ◄

tance he plants his potatoes in the row. The man who drops the potatoes has them in a basket or bag suspended from the shoulders and with this guide or spout in one hand he drops the potatoes through it, the end of the tail piece always resting on the last potato dropped. This little device secures perfect spacing and straight rows if they are furrowed straight. A second man follows with the fertilizer, dropping a spoonful a couple inches away from the seed piece, and a third man follows with hoe and covers. This spout can be made of round 3 in. tin pipe and I would suggest that the tail piece be fastened up four or six inches from the bottom to allow for irregularities in the bottom of the furrow. This device is not patented and so any who wish to make it can do so. I shall give a cut of it if it can be done in time to appear in the last pages to go to press.

The recent advent of the potato planter is to the potato grower what the mowing machine was to the dairyman and stock feeder, and is destined to soon become a common farm implement throughout our land of progressive and labor saving farmers.

AS TO CUTTING OF SEED

There are about as many practical growers for it as against it and the pet theories of each cover all degrees of size from large whole tubers down to single eye cuttings.

Here is a field for almost unlimited discussion and extended experiments. This is another place where it is hard to advise, the circumstances mainly, deciding the case. It would be a waste of money to pay a high price for a novelty in potatoes and plant whole tubers, and it probably would be unwise in most all cases to undertake to cut up fine seed which was only a little more expensive than potatoes to eat. On this subject the Experiment Stations have shed some light. Most of them agree in the conclusion that whole potatoes yield more per acre than cuttings under exactly the same circumstances. The large tuber furnishes nourishment to the young plant before it gets a large root development, thus enabling it to make a vigorous start at first ; whereas the cutting may be so small that it will dry up or get a week behind the other plant for lack of immediate nourishment and enough of it. One if not more of the Experiment Stations I believe has found in favor of cuttings in yield of marketable potatoes. Where the tests seem to be unfair is that a single eye is expected as much of alone by itself, three feet from a neighbor as of a large, whole tuber. If the tests were made with

I exhibited at only three Fairs the past Fall, but took a Premium at each one, on collection of Potatoes.

That this lock has more than passing merit, is shown by the fact that it had hardly been patented before the patentee was offered a fabulous sum for the rights of his i n v e n t i o n, which he however refused, being assured by old lock men that it was of extraordinary value and he would do better to m a n u facture it. He sold his foreign rights for a very respectable sum and has every encouragement that it is to have a very popular reception in this country.

One very neat device, in connection with the lock, is that when the door is open the catch or bolt is always in the lock and not sticking out as in common locks to catch clothing on or to make friction in shutting the door. See pages 16 and 18 for further information. Address all correspondence in regard to the lock to **G. D HOWE, North Hadley, Hampshire Co., Mass.,** who is the Co.'s special agent for its introduction and sale.

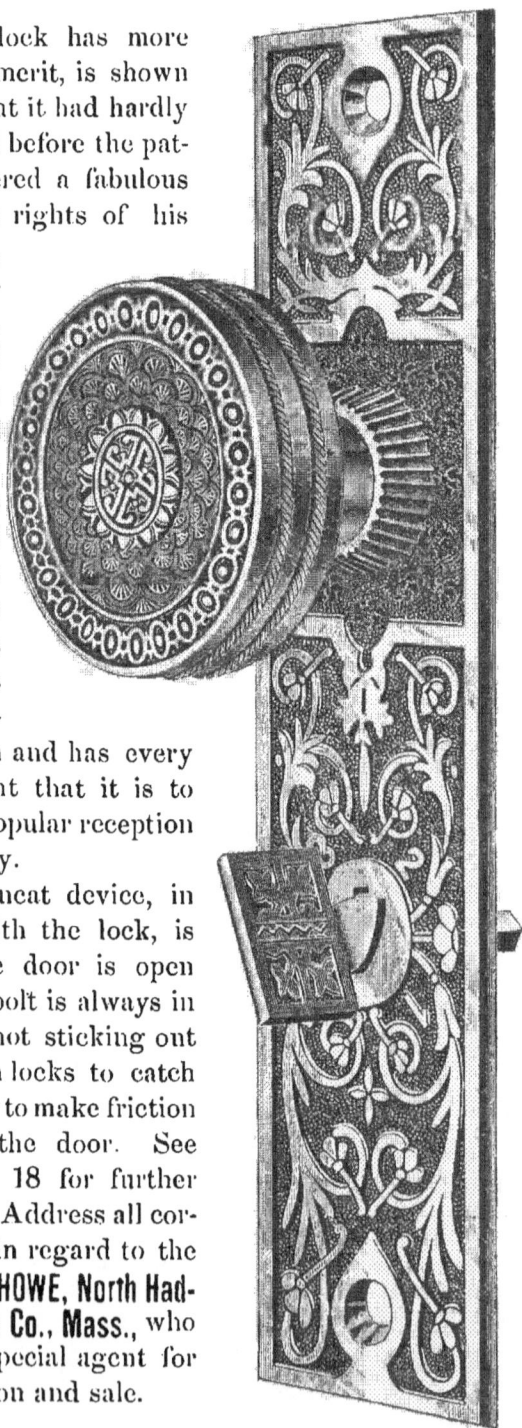

whole tubers planted two or three feet apart in the rows, and the single eyes eight to twelve inches apart. I think the single eye patch would make a creditable showing with the whole tuber patch, with very much lighter seeding at that.

The fact seem to be that whole tubers give a large total yield with a large per cent. of small potatoes, while with one or two eye cuttings the total yield may not be as great, but the yield of marketable potatoes is likely to be greater. One of the leading seed potato growers of the country plants only single eye cuttings. My entire crop last season was from single eye cuttings and got about fifteen bushels from a single half peck of seed of one variety. My average yield was between three and four hundred bushels per acre. Yet we can be sure of this fact from the tests of the Stations that the larger the seed piece attached to the eye the better plant it will make.

In the cultivation of the crop the great thing is to keep down the weeds and keep the soil mellow. There are many modern devices for cultivating, each probably with some particular merit, and from the large list to pick from, all of us ought to be pretty well satisfied. For small patches it is more convenient to apply paris green mixed with plaster through sieves made especially for the purpose, at the rate of from 50 to 100 bls. of plaster to a pound of the green, if it is pure, which ought to cover thoroughly a half acre to an acre of potatoes according to heaviness of seeding and size of tops. For a large field it is cheapest to drive through the field with a sprinkling cart, which keeps stirring the water all the time to prevent the poison from sinking to the bottom, as it is insoluble in water, and sprinkles several rows at a time and more effectually than plaster can do it if the flow of water is gauged correctly. About a teaspoonful of Paris green to a gallon of water.

As the leaves of the potato plant are as important to the development of the tuber as the lungs of a boy are to his growth, it is of the

ABOUT MY ADVERTISERS.

It has been my aim to admit only thoroughly reliable firms into my pages as advertisers. I have every reason to believe they will do just as they agree and prove perfectly satisfactory in any business relations you may have with them. As I wish to keep the standard of my Potato Manual high, I will be greatly obliged to any one, who finds dealings with any of them unsatisfactory, to let me know, and if their grievances prove well founded, I shall not admit that firm as an advertiser in future editions of the Manual. By doing this you will not only do me a favor, but also favor thousands of fellow farmers.

utmost importance that the bugs be kept, in subjection. As soon as
the tops are ripe, either from natural causes or disease, the tubers
will be better off in the cellar than in the ground.

So, unless selling for early market, when they are dry while the
tops are yet quite green, the next thing in order will be digging and
storing away.

As the only really successful diggers are pretty expensive, a farmer
who raises but an acre or two of potatoes will have to dig them by
the old fashioned back-breaking method, which, however, is thorough
if it is hard and slow. This is where the disadvantage of the small
grower comes in more than anywhere else. With several acres of
potatoes the owner could not afford to pass a single season without
one of the best potato diggers, and he will save money with it even
the first year.

If you are particular to have a very fine flavored potato, don't let
it lie exposed to the sun only just long enough to dry the surface.
Do not let it heat clear through as it must be cooled off again before
putting into bins or barrels in the cellar. Potatoes soon become
under the action of the sun like the leaves, green and bitter. Now
is the time to save out seed potatoes for another year, especially so
if digging by hand. When you come to an extra productive hill
throw out one side the largest ones, it won't hurt these for seed if
they do get sunburned a little.

To keep potatoes in fine condition they want to be kept perfectly
dormant ; some 10° above the freezing point all through the winter

"Popular Gardening and Fruit Growing."

This popular dollar horticultural monthly, published at Buffalo, N.
Y., is considered by the principal authorities as the leading journal
of its kind. It is certainly first-class in every respect ; what more
can you ask? For every new subscription to this journal sent through
my agency. I will give 40 cents worth of potatoes from this catalogue
or a year's subscription to the Farm Journal, Am. Farm News, or
Herds and Flocks..

Up to March 20, I will give it free to those who purchase
three dollars worth of potatoes, if new subscribers, and to old subscribers for an order for five dollars worth of potatoes.

I wish you would at least send for a sample copy of this paper,
which, though it costs ordinarily 10 cents, will be sent free by the
publishers if you state in your request that this offer was made in
Howe's Potato Manual. For sample copies address the publishers
as above and send your subscriptions to me.

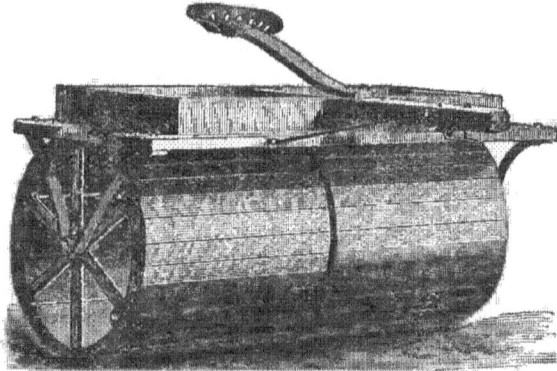

will bring them out in good shape in the spring either for seed or market. They want to be kept from draughts of air which shrivel them up, but not air tight which is apt to make them heat, mould and decay.

HOW TO SAVE A CROP FROM DROUGHT.

While we don't believe it would be practicable where potatoes are raised on a large scale, yet if you have a valuable small patch of potatoes which are promising much just as overtaken by drought they can probably be saved by mulching with that litter which is cheapest to apply.   Poor hay, straw, or such material that can be raked off if desired, will do.   Some potato growers have in years past, if they do not now, raised their whole crop in this way, as will be seen in another division of this pamphlet.

For extensive potato growers the following is about all that can be done profitably. *Cultivate thorough and often.* This method of action in drought is exactly the reverse of the old idea, but its correctness was investigated and substantiated by Hon. Levi Stockbridge of Amherst, Mass., while he was Professor in the Mass. Agricultural College, by a series of extensive and thorough experiments.

TO MY READER.

DEAR FRIEND,—I have gone to great expense to make your acquaintance and an equally great expense to hand you this manual and now why not remain friends? By becoming a patron, no matter for what or to what extent, you will receive next year's Manual which from the partial prospectus on page 31 you will want to see. I want every addressed envelope sent out, returned to me for some purpose. Will you find some use for the one I send you?

I would prefer each one to contain some money, but, if you can't find any other use for the envelope, let it inclose a list of a few of your friends who would be likely to be interested in the next Manual.

Don't send names of any persons who would probably not become my customers for something or other, as the publishing and mailing is a very expensive job, which expense however can be met by an order of some sort from every recipient of the book.

You might send this list of names even if you send an order, and I shall be pleased to send you some return for it.

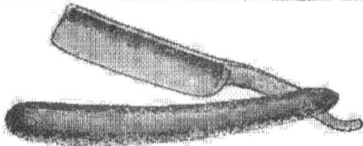

The idea is that in drought there is very rapid evaporation of water from the soil, through capilary tubes, in about the same manner as oil passes through a wick as it is burned by the flame on top, and if these tubes are continually disturped the evaporation is checked.

With these few thoughts on potatoes jotted down as they popped into the writer's head, he hopes the reader is sufficiently interested in the culture of fine potatoes to, at least, try a few hills of a kind if nothing more, to see how much poorer or better a new variety can be than the old one. If the new one proves poorer, then you will appreciate the old standby better and think of it every time it comes onto the table, and feel that the money invested to find out the value of the old was well spent; but if the new variety proves a pleasant innovation, then you will be doubly pleased and satisfied with the trial.

MISCELLANEOUS QUOTATIONS.

In the $100 Prize Essay, edited by Rev. W. T. Wylie, there are these quotations from an experienced cultivator, viz. :

" Secure the *best seed*, even if it costs you two or five times as much as a common and less valuable sort." "*Always* get a new, improved variety, as soon as it has been tested and proved. *Remember* the profit is mainly made by the early cultivators. When it gets so common that *you* can buy cheap, you will have to *sell* cheap, too."

Mr. Wylie in the same pamphlet gives the following.

How to double your crop when you have new and rare kinds.—In an ordinary hot bed or cold frame, put six inches of good, loose, rich soil ; split your potato and lay it cut side down about three inches under the surface, when the sprouts are four or five inches high, lift

GOOD BOOKS.

It is necessary for a gardner or farmer in order to keep up to the times, to read some good and standard books in his line of business in addition to his favorite agricultural paper. These books are apt to be the life long experiences of shrewd, successful and hard working men, and you can get your money's worth out of any of them. I will supply you with any book you want, if not sold by subscription, at 10 per cent. discount from the publishers' regular price. Be sure and give the name and price of book, its author and publishers.

If you want books on a certain subject and don't know of a book that just fills the bill, let me know your wants and perhaps I can help you.

the potato, slip off the sprouts and plant them. You can then cut the tuber into single eyes and plant as usual. The crop from the sprouts will ripen two weeks before the others. I made $40 this year by trying this with a *handful* of potatoes. Every reader is welcome to it and may make as much or more than I did, if he secures a few pounds of the newer and costly but valuable kinds.

D. H. Compton, in his prize essay says "Much is gained by changing seed. * * * Even when the same variety is desired, experience shows the great benefit of planting seed grown on a different soil. The best and most extensive growers procure new seed every two or three years, and many insist on changing seed every year; and undoubtedly the crop is often doubled by the practice.

READ THIS

And take the good advice. M. Crawford on Seed Catalogues.

"The following is taken from 'Gleanings in Bee Culture.' Mr. Crawford says to Mr. Root,—" When I get a bright new catalogue that evidently cost the seed grower quite a sum of money a piece, I have always had a sort of feeling that he deserved at least a little encouragement from every one who received it; therefore I mail a little order for onion seeds to our friend Maule; buy some new wax beans of Burfee; a few packets of Henderson and so on; and if I get the seeds, of course I must give them a little plat of ground.

These great red onions that you are admiring here were the product of Manle's strain of Wonderful Red; these great white ones are Burfee's Silver King, and so on. I have no particular use for them, growing strawberries mainly, as I do; but it gives me a feeling of pleasure, just as it does you, in this: that these new things are really what they are represented to be, and that they are certainly superior to the common King we have been selling."

Now, the above may not have been exactly friend C.'s words, but they are the sum and substance of them, and I do think that every one of you who receives one of these beautifully illustrated catalogues, with their colored plates, ought to send the proprietor at least a small order for seeds, by way of encouragement. If you pay 10 or 25 cts. for the catalogue, you need not make an order unless you choose; but where it is sent you free, I think you can pick out at least a few simple things that will be worth all they cost you, and at the same time prove an encouragement to the one who expends so much money in getting up the catalogue.

❋ PEKIN DUCK FARM. ❋

Our large flock of magnificent
breeders, selected with the greatest care
from over **8000** last spring ducklings. Began
laying in December, 1888. We are ready to supply
customers with eggs. Printed directions for hatching
and raising ducks accompany each order, if so
desired, for **$1.50** per dozen. Special
rates for filling incubators.

F. H. FAIRFIELD,

SUCCESSORS TO PETERS & CO.,

WALPOLE, MASS.

THE FLORIDA DESPATCH, FARMER ❧ FRUIT GROWER.

The Leading Agricultural Journal of the South.

PUBLISHED WEEKLY AT $2.00 PER YEAR.

Specimen Copies on application.

This Journal is a 24 page weekly of 96 columns. Is the official
organ of the Florida Farmers' Alliance; also the Florida Fruit and
and Vegetable Growers' Association; also endorsed by all as the
best thing of its kind in the South.

Address,

CHAS. W. DA KOSTA, PROPRIETOR,

JACKSONVILLE, FLA.

HOWE'S POTATO MANUAL FOR 1890.

I intend that next year's Manual shall be as much better and more interesting than this one as this is better than nothing. And to secure that end I *will pay you for your co-operation* as follows : From 10 cts. to $1.00 worth of potatoes from my next year's catalogue, according to the amount of trouble you go to and the apparent value of the information sent. Such as have a measure of success in growing potatoes can give their method of growing, harvesting and marketing. State particularly what fertilizers you use and how they are used and what quantity. State the quantity grown and the yield per acre, whether early or late, or if part of each what proportion. What varieties grown. What the character of the soil is, when the planting season begins, what the method of planting and cultivating is, quantity of seed used per acre and what tools are used, and, if particularly useful, where they are made. Any experience with seed, fertilizers, tools or methods that have proved unprofitable. State where your market is and average price obtained per bushel, and estimate how many bushels are grown in your town and how many in your county. Also any other information on the subject that will be likely to be of value in making up this little *Encyclopedia on the potato.*

All articles sent in will be acknowledged and the price allowed on them stated as soon as received. Probably none will be given credit after November 1, as that will leave none too much time to do the compiling before sending the matter to press.

No names will be used for publication without special permission. Send in the items as early as possible and on sheets of paper separate from all other business.

TO ADVERTISERS.

This Manual furnishes a peculiarly valuable advertising medium, its readers being obtained largely by advertising in the leading agricultural and other papers of the country at large, whose combined *actual subscribers* amount to *over a million, each issue.*

I wish to keep the standard of my Manual at the highest possible point such a publication can occupy, and shall make it a particular item to admit no advertisements of a *second rate,* to say nothing of those of a doubtful nature. Advertisements of this sort will not be admitted at any price.

My terms for the next issue will be very moderate, and any who would like to have the recommend an advt. in my Manual would give them, are requested to correspond with me about the matter before the first of October, if possible.

HOW TO SEND MONEY.

It is not safe to send coin, stamps, or postal notes in ordinary letters. While probably a thousand would come through all right, one might be tampered with. Do not take the risk, the best ways are, to send by bank drafts, P. O. Money Order, Express Money Order, and registered letter. The latter way is a little slow. If it is more convenient to send a common personal check than anything else, I will take that, but prefer one of the other methods. Have all money papers payable to my order. Do not send a check or draft that is not payable to me, with simply your name and nothing else endorsed on it as then it is only a little safer than so much coin in the letter; but write over your name "pay to the order of G. D. Howe." If sending a P. O. Money Order, have it payable at Northampton, Mass. To all those who send by either of the first three ways named above, I put in some 10c. premium, of my own selection. U. S. postage stamps of any denomination taken up to Mar. 15, after which send only one and two cent stamps. To those who are to send money loose in the envelope, if they will send by postal note instead, I will allow them a 5c. premium. No Canada stamps, coin or bills taken.

SPECIAL OFFERS AND PREMIUMS ON POTATOES, GOOD TILL MARCH 20.

1.—I will give five eyes of a variety of ten varieties of my own selection, either all early or all late or one half each for $1.00. These will be put up before the busy season which explains the low price.

2.—Except as noted on page 45, for an order for a dollars worth of potatoes I will give a years subscription to either of these papers described on pages 55 and 57,—No. 5, 23, 33, 34, 61 or 73.

3.—Except as noted on page 45, for an order for two dollars worth of potatoes I will give any two of the above papers or any one of the following, viz:—No. 9, 10, 15, 22, 24. 40, 44, 45, 48, 49, 55, 56. 62, 71, 75 or 76, or Western World Hand-book, mentioned on page 13.

4.—Except as noted on page 45, for an order for three dollars worth of potatoes, I will give any three of the papers offered under offer No. 2, or one of those and one from offer 3 or any one of the following papers;—No. 6, 11, 12, 13, 14, 17, 21, 25, 35, 36, 39, 51, 53, 54*, (see p. 23,) 57 or 60, or knife mentioned on page 59.

5.—Except as noted on page 45, for an order for four dollars worth of potatoes, I will give any combination of the foregoing of-

*To new subscribers only.

fers to make same value or any one of papers No. 2, 8, 19, 27, 38, 41, 47, 50, 58, 59, 67, 70 or 75.

6.—Except as noted on page 45, for an order for five dollars worth of potatoes, I will give any combination of the foregoing offers to make same value or any one of papers No. 1, 4, 7, 18, 20, 26, 32, 37, 46, 52, 64, 65, 66 or 69 or a copy of French's book by mail, advertised on page 4.

7.—Except as noted on page 45, for an order for six dollars worth of potatoes, I will give any combination of the foregoing to get same value or the scale mentioned on page 11 or either of these papers, No. 16, 28, 29, 31, 42*, 63, 68, 72 or 77.

8.—Except as noted on page 45, for a seven dollar order for potatoes, any combination of the foregoing offers for equal value or either of papers No. 3 or 43.

9.—Except as noted on page 45, for an eight dollar order for potatoes, any combination of the foregoing for equal value or paper No. 30.

10.—Except as noted on page 45, for a ten dollar potato order, the scales mentioned on page 15.

If your order amounts to over ten dollars write for special discount naming what you want. No discount on orders for ten dollars or less except by way of premiums as noted.

Cash must in all cases accompany the order, for no matter how well known you are commercially, I cannot afford to bother with personal ledger accounts at this time of the year.

The potatoes will be sent of course as soon in the spring as the weather will permit with safety, and the premiums immediately after the receipt of your order.

THE AMERICAN GARDEN.

RURAL KANSAN.

HOW I SELECT MY SEED STOCK.

The continued and careful experiments of the New York Experiment Station has led conclusively to the decision that Seed Potatoes can be bred or grown for productiveness by proper selection of seed stock. Their experiments were exhaustive on the subject, and the results are rational.

Their methods of experimenting to reach this conclusion, were to plant the largest tubers and smallest tubers from the most productive hills, by themselves, and the same division of the potatoes from the least productive hills of a certain patch.

In most instances the result of the smallest tubers from the most productive hills exceeded in yield those from the largest seed of the least productive hills. The yield of the largest tubers from the most productive hills exceeded by considerable the yield from the largest tubers of the least productive hills.

The principle is plain and reasonable. Why not improve your seed potato stock by selection as well as improve your herd of cows for milk, butter or beef, by selection?

To do this, it must be done at digging time, and of course all know it involves quite a little trouble and expense.

This is the way all my potatoes are selected for seed ; so, according to the results of the New York Experiment Station, even my small potatoes are worth more than common, unselected stock of large size.

Do you wonder that we have to get a little more for carefully raised seed potatoes than they are worth to eat.

Another thing of considerable consequence is the changing of seed stock, introducing seed grown in a different climate. I had seed potatoes from over a dozen different sources last year and in many cases direct from the originators and original introducers, to insure true stock. I shall continue to get new seed from reliable growers to compare with my own selected stock, including all the new varieties as fast as they are introduced, thus my customers can get of me the new varieties introduced by the various seedsmen, all in one package, and at money saving prices.

Many potato growers firmly believe it means dollars in their pocket to get seed grown away from their vicinity and do so for their entire crop every year. I know several common farmers who do this to say nothing of market men and specialists.

While I think there is considerable in this, yet I think the careful selection of most productive stock has more to do with it. But

5

whichever way you think, I can give you some satisfactory stock at the lowest possible prices consistent with thorough work.

I give you first a description of some of my best and cheapest varieties.

It wont always be the highest priced potato that will give you the best satisfaction, though it may be. You can only tell by actual trial which is best for you to grow, my poorest may be your best.

THE MONROE CO. PRIZE.

A very productive late variety. Shape, flattened, long and broad skin smooth and white ; very rank grower.

A single hill I pulled up at random last fall had seventeen tubers in it, fourteen of which were marketable, and the largest weighing about a pound a piece. The tops when straightened out were five feet long and all this with the hills a foot apart in the row and seed cut to single eyes.

The seed from which I raised my stock came direct from the introducers and I have a fine lot to offer. As will be seen by the table at the end of the book this variety stands high in order of yield in competitive trials for yield, at different stations. While one of the very best yielders it is at the same time very fine in quality.

Prices : 20 cts. per lb. by mail ; by express or freight, 10 cts. per lb. ; 65 cts. per pk. ; $2.00 per bu. ; $5.00 per bbl.

MONROE CO. PRIZE.

THE WHITE SEEDLING.

This sterling late variety gave the best of satisfaction on my grounds last season. It is an enormous grower and proportionate yielder. It resembles very closely in all respects the Monroe Co. Prize. It is rather more smooth and a little more regularly shaped than that variety. It seems to be perfectly hardy and vigorous. Reports seem to indicate that both the Monroe and this are a considerable improvement on two of the present leading late potatoes, viz.: White Star and Burbank. It is very white and cooks beautifully. An examination of the tables of comparative yield in the back part of this manual will show how high it stands in this requisite. It was one of my most productive sorts the past season.

Prices same as for Monroe Co. Prize.

Bbls. are for three measured bushels, or 2¾ weighed 165 lbs.

WHITE SEEDLING.

It is very probable that the stock of some of the varieties I grew may become exhausted early in the season, so it will save much time if you will say whether I am at liberty to substitute another variety or not. If nothing is said about it and there is not time to correspond about the matter, I shall act according to the best of my judgement in the matter being governed somewhat by the wording of the order. In all cases where it is apparent that you just what is ordered or nothing, it I am out of that variety the money will be immediately returned.

THE CHARLES DOWNING.

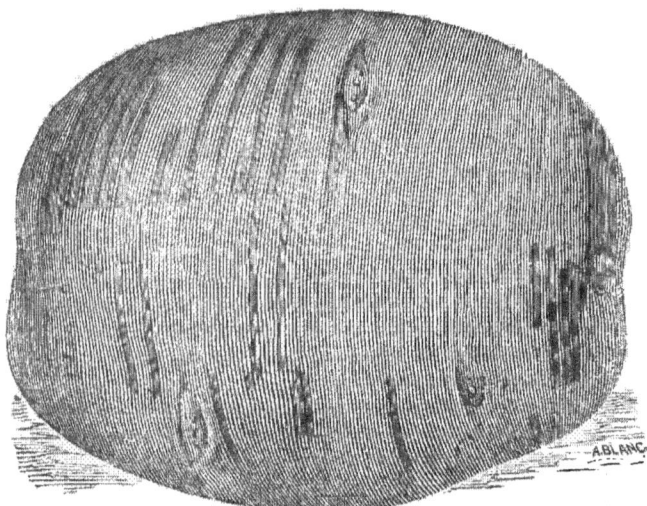

The Charles Downing potato originated in Vermont and is of the Snowflake type. In most sections of the country it has proven an extra yielder, as well as being early and of the very first quality. The pototoes are what most people would call of model shape for cooking purposes, flat-oval, with eyes very scarce and shallow. Many tubers can be found with only one eye on a whole side. With me it yielded at the rate of 336 bushels per acre last year. The tubers are rather scattering in the hill, tops medium heavy. It has proved in some portions to be more susceptible to blight than other varieties and has been therefore condemned. But wherever the soil and climate are right it will be a first-class potato for both market and home use. If you are fastideous about your potatoes this one will suit. At a test of over one hundred varieties at the Ohio Agricultural Experiment Station a few years ago, this and the Snowflake were the only ones marked the maximum in quality. In the same test is proved to be one of the best yielders.

Prices : 20 cts. per lb. by mail,   By express or freight, 10 lbs. at 65 cts. per peck ; $2.00 per bushel; $5.00 per barrel.

Our nearest shipping point is Hadley on the Central Mass. R. R., a division of the Boston & Maine R. R., though we can ship from Northampton by the Conn. River R. R. or the N. Y., N. H. and Hartford R. R., or from Amherst by the Central Vt. R. R.

All prices herein given are for goods (which are not sent by mail), packed and delivered at express office or R. R. station free.

LEE'S FAVORITE.

Is one of the few new varieties that seem to have come to stay. Its popularity is rapidly increasing for various substantial reasons. It is very early, productive and hardy. With me it yielded 346 bu. per acre the past year. While I don't con sider it quite as fine in quality as the Downing, it certain- y is excellent. The shape of the tuber is not so handsome or taking as the Downing, but still I am inclined to think it will outrival that variety in popularity taking them the country over.

The Ohio Experiment Station for 1885 showed it to outyield about 100 other sorts by quite a handsome lead.

Its shape is long and a little flattened. Color, flesh, pink at the eye and on the end. One of the leading Chicago dealers told me last summer that this variety sold best of any early sort.

TRUE POTATO SEED.

I gathered a quantity of the true potato seed last summer from my varieties, and by particular care that it thoroughly ripened before curing, I offer it in packets of about 50 seeds in a packet, with the name of the variety from which gathered, at 20 cents per packet. Most dealers ask 25 cents per packet of 25 seeds.

Directions for culture accompany each packet.

Try a packet, it will be interesting to see the great variety you will get, some of which may prove very valuable, in which case it will be a little gold mine for a year or two.

THE EARLY PURITAN.

The Early Puritan was originated by Mr. E. L. Coy, of Washington Co., New York, of Beauty of Hebron fame. It was introduced last year by Messrs. Henderson & Co., of New York. This variety promises very much. It is one of the best in quality, a good yielder, tops very small, tubers very compact in the hill, making very handsome digging, and it is hardy. I think so much of it that I shall raise a large quantity this year. One thing worth noting is its rot resisting quality. In my village there was a patch of Beauty of Hebrons on rich land and beside it on still richer soil of the same nature was a patch of these Early Puritans. They were all harvested about the same time with about half the Hebrons decayed and hardly a poor Puritan in the lot. They are long, not flat, white and have rather large eyes.

Prices : 3o cts. per lb. by mail ; by express or freight, 20 cts. per lb., 90 cts. per peck. $2.75 per bushel, $7.00 per barral.

EARLY SUNRISE.

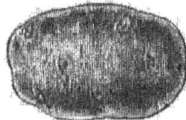

Early Sunrise, is of the rose class, a medium long, handsome potato. Excellent quality. very early.

No. 131.   Prices, 25c. per lb. by mail ; by express or freight, 15c, per lb., 50c. per peck, $1.75 per bushel, $4.50 per barrel.

THE NEW QUEEN.

The New Queen is a very productive new sort, of fine quality.   It

was first introduced only two or three years ago and is a seedling of
the Beauty of Hebron. It is very highly commended on all sides.
No. 159. Prices, 25c. per lb. by mail. By express or freight,
15c. per lb., 65c. per peck, $2.00 per bushel, $5.00 per barrel.

POTATO EYES.

For the price of potato eyes, cut scientifically, with liberal pieces
of the tuber attached to each eye, substitute 10 eyes for the word
pound and you have it. These will be only strong, healthy pieces
and of extra size, so that each plant will be vigorous and sizable.
These figures are rock bottom and far below the prices of seedsmen.
It is only because I am in the business and grow my own seed that
enables me to offer them so reasonable. If anyone offers cuttings
cheaper you may be assured they are small pieces and not worth
half what mine are to make strong plants. I had some last year
from different seedsmen that were not larger than cents and not
much thicker. Such eyes will not give the satisfaction that mine
will.

I don't care to put up less than 5 eyes of a variety, and less than
that number will be charged at 5 eye rate. 120 eyes of a kind
given for the price of 100.

The advantage of buying the eyes by mail is that you can get
started with several new varieties of potatoes at a very small cost,
and then you get only the very best eyes, as I shall sell no end pieces
for cuttings, and they arrive all cut ready for planting, and that done
better than you would be likely to do it. Five eyes ought to yield
you, with only ordinary care, from a half peck to a peck of seed for
another year. Then a half peck cut to single eyes ought to give you
from five to ten bushels, and that would be enough to plant from two
to five acres. These calculations are based upon my own results in
the past. After you had tried the different kinds the three years
you could readily tell which one or two were best adapted to your
soil, climate and market, and could discard the others.

A FEW OF MY VARIETIES.

For the following 138 varieties, price 15 cts. per pound by express
or freight, and 25 cts. per pound by mail.

NO.		NO.	
51.	Adirondac.	60.	Mayflower.
18.	Albino.	50.	Mitchell's Seedling.
69.	Alexander's, No. 1.	117.	Morning Star.
126.	" Prolific.	90.	Mullally.
97.	Astonisher.	46.	Nevada White.
39.	Baker's Imperial.	101.	New Champion.
26.	Barstow.	38.	New York State.
122.	Beauty of Hebron.	159.	New Queen.
36.	" " Late.	41.	Newton's Seedling.
161.	Beauty of Beauties, Rose's.	82.	Nott's Victor.
119.	Belle.	129.	O. K. Mammoth Prolific.
/%	Blaine, Jas. G.	45.	Ontario.
91.	Bonanza.	61.	Orange Co. White.
21	Boston Market.	107.	Parson's Prolific.
92.	Brownell's Best.	164.	Peachblow.
68.	" No. 31.	116.	Pearl of Savoy.
111.	" No. 55.	30.	Perfect Gem.
27.	Cambridge Prolific.	35.	Perfection, Finch's.
110.	Carter.	155.	Potentate.
10.	Cayuga.	63.	Prairie Farmer.
86.	Champlain.	56.	Pride of Lisbon.
93.	Charter Oak.	98.	Pride of the West.
54.	Cheesman's Seedling.	11.	Prince Edward Island Rose.
102.	Chicago Gem.	15.	Princess.
80.	Clark's No. 1.	108.	Putnam.
83.	Collum's Superb.	79.	Queen of the Roses.
77.	Corliss' Matchless.	71.	Queen of the Valley.
104.	Crane's Extra Keeper.	95.	Ricker's Graft.
44.	" June Eating.	53.	Rhinebeck.
32.	Cream of the Field.	67.	Rochester Favorite.
105.	Crimson Beauty.	73.	Rose's Invincible.
152.	Crown Jewel.	81.	Rose's No. 71.
64.	Dakota Red.	78.	Rosy Morn.
49	Dakota White.	4.	Rubicund.
157.	Dandy.	124.	Rural Blush.
133.	Delaware	99.	Rural Buttercup.
29.	Dictator	55.	Salt Lake Queen.
6.	Duchess.	112.	Seneca Red Jacket.
115.	Early Essex.	22.	Sheridan, General.
20.	Early Dawn.	57.	Silver Skin.
2.	Early Durham.	84.	Snowbank, Knopp's.
151.	Early Gem.	58.	Spaulding
33.	Early Harvest.	85.	Summit.
113.	Early Maine.	127.	Sunlit Star.
165.	Early Mayflower.	52.	Stanton.
19.	Early New Zeland.	7.	State of Maine.
75.	Early Pearl.	25.	Steuben Beauty.
168.	Early Rose (true pedigree stock).	87.	Steuben Chief.
131.	Early Sunrise.	121.	Stray Beauty.
162.	Early Standard.	43.	Storr's Seedling.
5.	Early White Prize.	3.	Sylvan.
70.	El Paso.	62.	Thunderbolt.
120.	Empire State.	128.	Thornburn.
100.	Eno's Seedling.	17.	Triumph, Bliss'
94.	Garfield, Burrough's.	16.	Tunix.
14.	" Landreth's.	89.	Vanguard
59.	Great Eastern.	42.	Vick, James.
70.	Green Mountain.	156.	Victory.
160.	Golden Flesh.	40.	Weld's No. 14.
123.	Hampden Beauty.	34.	" No. 22.
9.	Jumbo, Weld's.	66.	" No. 40.
74.	Junkis.	24.	White Chief.
		125.	White Elephant.

A FEW OF THE NOVELTIES.

BURPEE'S SUPERIOR.

This late potato, introduced this year for the first time, is a seedling of the White Star. It is highly praised as a main cropper and is said to withstand the new (to many of the Eastern States) potato pest, the flea beetle, better than other sorts.

It originated with E. L. Coy, the celebrated potato specialist.

The only objection I can find against it is the depth at which it grows its tuber, which are also scattered thus adding to the expense of digging.

Prices, by mail, 50 cts. per lb., 3 lbs. $1.25 ; by freight or express, 40 cts. per lb. ; $1.25 per peck, $4.00 per bushel, $8.50 per barrel, two barrels or more $8.00 per barrel.

EARLY MARKET (VICK'S).

This new potato introduced this year by James Vick is of the Ohio class, and it is claimed by him to be one of the earliest and best of that family. Its particular feature being its edible qualities before ripening. It is long and round, with small specks on the skin, and the tubers grow compact in the hill.

Prices : 75 cts. per lb. by mail ; by express or freight, 65 cts. per lb. : $1.50 per peck, $5.00 per bushel, $10.00 per barrel.

6

RURAL NEW YORKER NO. 2.

Introduced this year by James M. Thorburn & Co. Originated at the experimental grounds of "The Rural New Yorker." It is highly praised and undoubtedly very valuable. At the famous test last season at the Rural grounds, it resisted the flea beetle best of the sorts tried and yielded at the rate of over a thousand bushels per acre. It is intermediate in ripening.

Prices : 60 cts. per lb., 3 lbs. $1.50 by mail ; by freight or express 50 cts. per lb., ½ peck $1.50, 1 peck $2.50, ½ bushel $4.00, per bushel $7.00, per barrel $15.00.

THE MINISTER (JERRARD'S.)

This is a very early sort introduced this year by Mr. Jerrard. It is very white and claimed to be extra good, while the vines are still green. It is noticeably rot resisting.

Prices : by mail 65 cts. per lb., 2 lbs. $1.25, 3 lbs. $1.65 ; by express or freight 50 cts. per lb., ½ peck $1.25, 1 peck $2.50, ½ bushel $4.00, 1 bushel $8.00.

DANDY.

This variety was introduced last year and is quite valuable. A very white sort, medium to late. A seedling of the Chenango.

Price : $1.25 per peck, $3.50 per bushel, $7.00 per barrel.

CHILD'S NORTH POLE.

Very early ; by mail, tubers 15 cts. each, 4 for 50 cts, $1.50 a doz. ; by express, $1.00 per doz., $8.00 per hundred.

BLACK MINORCAS.

This rather new breed (for this country) is one of the best for laying qualities. They are equal to the Leghorns in that respect, laying a large white egg. When you get ready to kill one you will find considerable meat on it. They have the largest combs of any breed, and where they can be kept warm will give abundant satisfaction. My stock is excellent. **Price, $1.50 per sitting or two sittings in same package, $2.50**

WHITE WYANDOTTES.

These are a sport of the laced wyandottes, and are like them in every detail except color. I have a very fine pen of these fowls which cost the breeder I procured them of $8.00 a piece. A limited number of sittings at $2.00 per sitting or two in same package, $3.00.

LACED (THE ORIGINAL) WYANDOTTES.

I shall have a few sittings of this variety to spare at $1.00 per sitting, two sittings in same package, $1.50. The Wyandotts and the Plymouth Rocks are the two leading American breeds.

SINGLE COMB BROWN LEGHORNS.

A well known breed of layers. $1.00 per sitting, two sittings in same package, $1.50.

PEKIN DUCKS.

The largest bodied and best layers of the duck family. They will convert a given amount of food into flesh quicker than anything else in the line of poultry, being ready for market in from six to eight weeks from the shell. $1.00 per sitting (of 11 eggs), two sittings in same package. $1.50.

CROSSES.

For solely practical, everyday use, many believe that crosses of thoroughbreds are much superior to their more aristocratic cousins.

You can get some thoroughbreds to take the prizes at your local fairs and some crosses to stay at home and work.

To suit such as want them I have arranged two admirable crosses for the very best results.

No. 1. Rose Comb White Leghorn cockerel and Light Brahma hens. 75 cts. per sitting, two in same package, $1.25.

No. 2. Single Comb Brown Leghorn cockerel and Partridge Cochin pullets. Prices same as for No. 1.

Each of these matings is designed for a practical result combining size, laying qualities, gentleness, activity and quick development.

In this matter of crossing it is asserted by the best authorities who have experimented in this line, that to get the best results, thoroughbreds must in all cases be used and not the product of the cross for subsequent breeding.

I shall use the greatest care to send out only the best eggs I can produce, and shall mark each egg with rubber stamp to check against meddling while in transit, as some unexplainable results sometimes occur with thoroughbred eggs shipped for hatching. I shall pack as carefully as I know how with an eye to security and lightness of package. When package is started on its journey my responsibilities will cease, and in no case, at the price I charge, shall I make good a poor hatch. Any apparent mistakes on my part will be rectified cheerfully at all times. If you do not care to buy on these terms, I do not care to sell.

☞See my advertisers for a higher grade of stock in the line of poultry.

CLUBBING LIST.

A. Frequency of issue.—w, weekly, s-m, semi-monthly, m, monthly, q, quarterly.

B. Size of page.

C. What the paper is devoted to.—1, General Agriculture. 2, Poultry. 3, Bees. 4, Horticulture. 5, Live Stock. 6, Family. 7, Floriculture. 8, Politics.
This classification is not in all cases fine but will give a general idea of the paper.

D. Number of pages.

E. Quality of paper on which printed and general appearance of the publication, three grades. This is not intended to be fine but to give only a general impression.
Nos. 2, 16, 17, 21, 22, 23, 30, 38, 41, 52, 55, 60, 61, 63 and 76 come uncut, all the others are cut so as to turn the pages as with a book.

F. Publishers price per year.
Nos. 18, 33, 40, 44, 49, 56 and 64 I did not have on hand when making up my descriptions and so cannot say as to them. Their size, etc., is taken from Ayer's Newspaper Annual for 1888. The descriptions of all the others are taken right from the papers which I have on file.

I take all the papers on my list and so can inform you at any time in regard to any of them. The size of No. 40 I cannot give as it has recently been made up by consolidations of other papers. The original of this was I. F. & Stockman, m. 10x13, 24p. $1.00 yr.

With a very few exceptions, I can supply any paper or magazine published at 10 per cent. discount from the publisher's price. You can remit at that rate, and if I cannot supply you, I will return the money with the additional cost of the postage on the letter to me, and if the wholesale price is low enough to admit, I will send you some premium extra.

Of the papers on my list, the discount will be only 5 per cent. on No. 1, 3, 46 and, 75 and on renewals to Nos. 42 and 54. Renewals to 77 will be at full list price.

No.	Name.	A.	B.	C.	D.	Where published.	E.	F.
1.	American Bee Journal,	w,	8x11,	3,	16,	Chicago, Ill.,	3,	$1 00
2.	American Breeder,	m.	10x14,	5,	36,	De Kalb, Ill.,	1,	1 00
3.	American Cultivator,	w,	18x24,	1,	8,	Boston, Mass.,	2,	2 00
4.	American Dairyman,	w,	11x14,	5,	8,	New York, N. Y.,	3,	1 50
5.	American Farm News,	m,	11x14,	6-1,	16,	Akron, O.,	1,	25
6.	American Poultry Journal,	m,	8x11,	2,	38,	Chicago, Ill.,	1,	1 00
7.	American Poultry Yard,	w,	16x22,	2,	4,	Hartford, Conn.,	3,	1 50
8.	American Rural Home,	w,	16x23,	6-1,	8,	Rochester, N. Y.,	3,	1 00
9.	American Swineherd,	m,	8x12,	5,	20,	Alexandria, Dak.,	3,	50
10.	Bee-Hive,	m,	6x9,	3,	12,	Andover, Conn.,	3,	25
11.	Bee Keeper's Advance,	m.	6x9,	3-2,	32	Mechanic Falls, Me.,	3,	50
12.	Bee-Keepers' Guide,	m,	6x9,	3,	32,	Kendallville, Ind.,	2,	50
13.	Bee-Keepers' Review,	m.	6x9,	3,	16,	Flint, Mich.,	3,	50
14.	California Cackler,	m,	9x12.	2,	22,	San Francisco, Cal.,	2,	1 00
15.	City and Country,	m,	11x15,	6,	16,	Columbus, O.,	2,	50
16.	Colorado Live Stock Review,	w,	11x20,	1-6,	8,	Pueblo, Colo.,	3,	2 00
17.	Cornucopia,	m,	11x16,	6,	8,	Norfolk, Va.,	3,	50
18.	Delaware Farm and Home,	w,	26x40,	1-6,	8,	Wilmington, Del.		1 00
19.	Fanciers Gazette,	m,	8x11,	2,	44,	Indianapolis, Ind.,	2,	1 25
20.	Farm, Field and Stockman,	w,	11x15,	1-5,	16,	Chicago, Ill.,	1,	1 00
21.	Farm and Fireside,	s-m,	11x15,	1-6,	16,	Springfield, O.,	3,	50
22.	Farm and Garden,	q,	11x14,	4,	16,	Thorn Hill, N. Y.,	3,	25
23.	Farm Journal,	m,	9x12,	1,	20,	Philadelphia, Pa.,	2,	50
24.	Farm Journal,	m,	10x14,	1-6,	16,	Richmond, Va.,	3,	50
25.	Farmer's Home,	m,	11x16,	1,	12,	Dayton, O.,	2,	50
26.	Farmers Home Journal,	w,	17x22,	1-5,	8,	Louisville, Ky.,	2,	1 50
27.	Farmers' Voice,	w,	10x13,	6,	28,	Chicago, Ill.,	3,	1 00
28.	Florida Agriculturist,	w,	11x15,	1,	16,	DeLand, Fla.,	3,	2 00
29.	Florida Dispatch,	w,	10x13,	1,	24,	Jacksonville, Fla.,	3,	2 00
30.	Garden and Forest,	w,	9x12,	4,	18,	New York, N. Y.,	1,	1 00
31.	Germantown Telegraph,	w,	23x31,	1-6,	4,	Germantown, Pa.,	3,	2 00
32.	Gleanings in Bee Culture,	s-m,	8x10,	3,	36,	Medina, O.,	1,	1 00

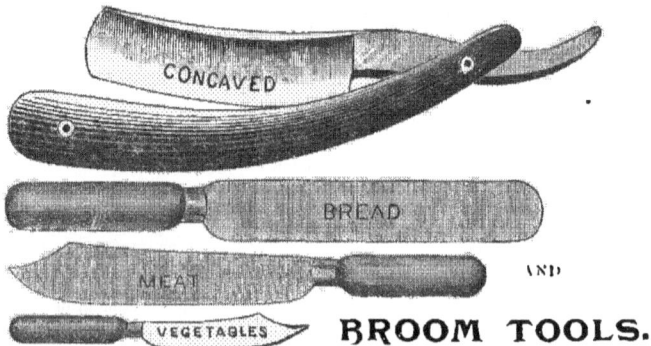

BROOM TOOLS.

MANUFACTURED BY

C. D. DICKINSON & SON,

NORTH HADLEY, MASS.

Established 1840.

THAT OLD RAZOR!!

We make new razors, but advise you not to throw away that old razor. Perhaps it is better than any new one you can get. Send it to us. *by mail,* together with 30, 40, 50, 60 or 70 cents and we will grind, hone and strop it and return it by mail in a condition that will please you. The amount of work we put on the razor will be according to the amount of money sent. 30 cents will secure considerable grinding, mostly at the edge, and a good cutting edge, set ready for use, provided the razor is susceptible to taking an edge. 70 cts. will secure a full concave, highly polished to a large razor, beside honing and stropping. There is less work on a small razor than a large one, so the same amount of money will go farther on a small than on a large one.

For common home use we do not advise a full concave, especially so if the beard is stiff and hard.

☞To send a razor by mail inclose in a tin case or *wind with wire.* If you have no wire and can't get it conveniently send us word by postal and we will send you some by return mail, suitable for the purpose.

We make also all kinds of Broom Tools, Kitchen Cutlery, Cigar Knives, Shoe Knives, Photographer's Knives, and any fine edged tools to order from sample or drawing.

All new goods sent out warranted to do what they ought to do.

C. D. DICKINSON & SON, North Hadley, Mass.

No.	Name.	A.	B.	C.	D.	Where published.	E.	F.
33.	Green's Fruit Grower,	q,	30x46,	4,	8,	Rochester, N. Y.,		50
34.	Herds and Flocks,	s-m,	9x12,	5,	16,	Chicago, Ill.,	1,	1 00
35.	Home and Farm,	s-m,	17x24,	6-1,	8,	Louisville, Ky.,	3,	50
36.	Home, Farm and Factory,	m,	11x15,	6,	12,	St. Louis, Mo.,	2,	50
37.	Holstein-Friesian Register,	s-m,	9x12,	5,	16,	Brattleboro, Vt.,	1,	1 50
38.	Housekeeper,	s-m,	11x16,	6,	16,	Minneapolis, Minn.,	3,	1 00
39.	Housewife,	m,	11x14,	6,	24,	Greenfield, Mass.,	3,	50
40.	Iowa Farmer and Breeder,			1-5,		Cedar Rapids, Iowa,		50
41.	Live-Stock Indicator,	w,	15x22,	5,	8,	Kansas City, Mo.,	3,	1 00
42.	Massachusetts Ploughman,	w,	18x23,	1,	8,	Boston, Mass.,	2,	2 00
43.	Montana Live-Stock Journal,	w,	15x21,	5-6,	16,	Helena, Montana,	3,	3 00
44.	National Farm and Fireside,	s-m,	11x15,	1,	16,	Washington, D. C.,		50
45.	New England Fancier,	m,	10x12,	2,	20,	Danielsonville, Conn.,	2,	50
46.	Ohio Farmer,	w,	11x16,	1,	24,	Cleveland, O.,	2,	1 00
47.	Ohio Poultry Journal,	m,	9x12,	2,	28,	Dayton, O.,	1,	1 00
48.	Ohio Swine Journal,*	m,	6x9,	5,	18,	Dayton, O.,	2,	50
49.	Ohio Valley Farmer,	m,	11x15,	1,	12,	Wheeling, W. Va.,		50
50.	Orange Judd Farmer,	w,	11x16,	1,	24,	Chicago, Ill.,	1,	1 00
51.	Orchard and Garden,	m,	9x12,	4,	24,	Little Silver, N. J.,	1,	50
52.	Pacific Farmer,	w,	10x12,	1-6,	16,	Portland, Oregon,	3,	2 00
53.	Park's Floral Magazine,	m,	6x9,	7,	16,	Fannettsburg, Pa.,	2,	50
54.	Popular Gardening,	m,	9x12,	4	16,	Buffalo, N. Y.,	1,	1 00
55.	Poultry Bulletin,	m,	9x12,	2,	46,	New York, N. Y.,	1,	50
56.	Poultry Herald,	m,	9x12,	2,	8,	St. Paul, Minn.,	2,	35
57.	Poultry Keeper,	m,	9x12,	2,	16,	Parkersburg, Pa.,		50
58.	Poultry Monthly,	m,	9x11,	2,	56,	Albany, N. Y.,	1,	1 25
59.	Poultry World,	m,	9x11,	2,	56,	Hartford, Conn.,	1,	1 25
60.	Poultryman,	m,	8x11,	2,	8,	Boston, Mass.,	2,	50
61.	Rays of Light,	m,	11x16,	2-3,	8,	N. Manchester, Ind.,	3,	25
62.	Rural Long Islander,	q,	15x25,	2-6,	8,	Stony Brook, N. Y.,	3,	25
63.	Rural New-Yorker,	w,	11x16,	1,	16,	New York, N. Y.,	1,	2 00
64.	Rural and Workman,	w,	11x14,	1,	16,	Little Rock, Ark.,	2,	1 50
65.	Santa Clara Valley,	m,	10x14,	4,	20,	San Jose, Cal.,		1 50
66.	Statesman,	m,	6x9,	6-8,	72,	Chicago, Ill.,	1,	2 00
67.	Stock Farmer,	m,	6x9,	5,	52,	Fort Worth, Texas,	3,	1 00
68.	Sugar-Bowl and Farm Journal,	w,	11x14,	1,	21,	New Orleans, La.,	2,	2 00
69.	Texas Live-Stock Journal,	w,	10x14,	5,	16,	Fort Worth, Texas,	3,	1 50
70.	Western Agriculturist,	m,	9x12,	5,	40,	Quincy, Ill.,	2,	1 10
71.	Western Farmer and Stockman,	m,	11x16,	1,	16,	Sioux City, Iowa,	3,	50
72.	W. Sportsman & Live-Stock News,	w,	11x15,	5,	20,	Indianapolis, Ind.,	3,	2 00
73.	W. Tree Planter & Fruit Grower,	m,	11x15,	4,	8,	Elgin, Ill.,	3,	50
74.	Western World,	q,	11x15,	6,	16,	Chicago, Ill.,	1,	25
75.	Wheel-Enterprise and Stockman,	w,	15x22,	1,	8,	Little Rock, Arks.,	3,	1 00
76.	Wisconsin Agriculturist,	m,	11x15,	1-6,	16,	Racine, Wis.	3,	50
77.	Youth's Companion,	w,	12x16,	6,	12,	Boston, Mass.,	1,	1 75

*Form and size to be changed

If you want to know more of this $7 fruit and vegetable evaporator write for special circulars of it.

I will give you any dollar newspaper or one of many $2.00 papers with the machine if ordered of me. If you once use it you will not get along without one in the future. See larger notice on another page.

MILL OR FACTORY SITE

WITH GOOD WATER POWER

TO RENT

What has for about two hundred years been the profitable saw mill site in North Hadley, Mass., is now, from various good reasons, not paying property. The wood lots have been cleared to stay, and only a few logs of the farmers make the winter's business of this mill. The building (30x100 feet) was built very strongly about thirteen years ago. There is about a quarter of an acre of yard room where other buildings could be erected to suit the business.

This can be secured for a very small rental fee.

As to the location, the village, which is one of the prettiest in New England, is a part of the town of Hadley. It is at the west foot of Mt. Warner, and on the east bank of the, Connecticut river, and seven miles north of Mt. Holyoke. Amherst, where are Amherst Amherst College, the Mass. Agricultural College and several private schools, is four miles to the east and Northampton, with its Smith College and many other institutions, is six miles to the south west. We are half way between Springfield and Greenfield, and about a hundred miles west of Boston. It is three miles to the depot on the Central Mass. R. R.,four miles to depot of another R. R. in Amherst and six miles to two other R. R. in Northampton.

House rent and cost of supplies are very low and so labor can be employed at a low figure, thus saving a large sum annually to any concern over a location in a large place.

The Grist Mill on the opposite side of the stream does a prosperous business, and the surplus power of the fifty acre mill pond could just as well turn other water wheels before going to Holyoke to convert saw logs into paper.

For further particulars address or inquire of the proprietor,

J. C. HOWE, North Hadley, Mass.

PREMIUMS ON PAPERS.

The following premiums offered on papers in my list are for them at publisher's prices.

Potatoes offered only till March 20. All other premiums hold good till another notice supercedes this. For any paper in the list I will give 10c. worth of potatoes from my catalogue, or three months' subscription to paper No. 55. In addition to the above, on papers No. 2, 4, 6 to 9 (inclusive), 14 to 16, 19, 23, 24, 26 to 31, 33, 34, 36 to 38, 40, 41, 42*, 43, 47 to 50, 52, 54*, 58, 59, 63 to 69, 71 to 73, and 77* I will give 10c. worth of potatoes from my catalogue, or three months' subscription to either of papers 14 or 55, or one year's subscription to either papers 23 or 33 with its premium.

In addition to the above, on papers No. 4*, 6, 7, 16, 19, 23, 26* 28 to 31, 34, 38, 42*, 43, 47, 52, 54*, 58, 59, 63 to 69, 72 and 73, I will give 10c. worth of potatoes from my list, or three months' subscription to either paper 14 or 55, or a year's subscription to 33 with its premium.

In addition to the above, on papers No. 30, 31*, 34, 52 and 66, I will give 10c. worth of potatoes from my catalogue or three months' subscription to either papers 14 or 55, or one year's subscription to either papers 5, 33 with its premium, or 34.

In addition to the above, on papers 30, 31*, and 34, I will give 10c. worth of potatoes or a year's subscription to 54*.

All these offers are for the papers without any other premiums, except 15, 17, 33 and 66, where publisher's premiums go with papers without extra cost. Any of the papers' regular premiums can be had by sending the amount extra, charged by the publishers for them.

*For new subscribers only.

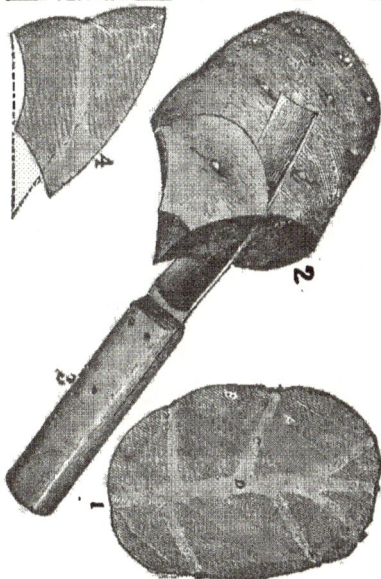

The Concaved and Curved Seed Potato Knife.

No one who cuts seed potatoes at all can afford to be without one of these knives. The illustration explains itself and will show that by using this knife the seed piece is left in the best possible shape to begin growing. They are made very thin and will work beautifully Furnished for either left or right handed people at 35 cts. each, postpaid.

I will include one, free with each three dollar order for potatoes where no other premium is given.

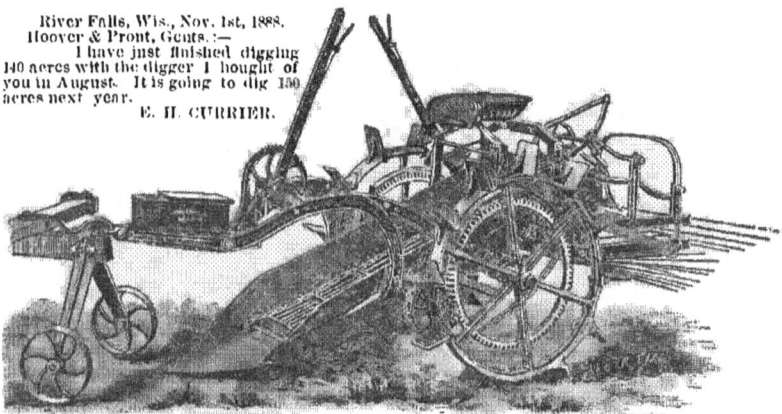

BOOKS RECEIVED.

American Newspaper Annual for 1888. Published by N. W. Ayer & Son, of Philadelphia, Pa., price $5.00. A 7x10 book of over a thousand pages. Statistics and all general information about newspapers and periodicals of America. It is the standard.

"Hand-Book of Volapük," by Chas. E. Sprague, 1271 B.oadway, New York City. A neat book of 120 5x7 pages, on heavy paper. The author is probably the highest authority on this new world-language in this country, price $1.00.

"Practical Poultry Keeping" and "Poultry for Pleasure and Poultry for Profit," bound together by G. M. T. Johnson of Binghampton, N. Y., price $1.00, size 4½x7. 120 and 48 pages. A book well illustrated and well written by an author who has had experience in what he writes of.

Two pamphlets on Carp Culture, by Milton P. Peirce now of Columbus. O. Capt. Peirce is probably the highest authority in the country on Carp culture, if not Fish culture in general. Such as have a small stream of water which could be utilized for a carp pond will do well to interest themselves in this subject by corresponding with Capt. Peirce.

Preston's Wyandotte Gazette, by Geo. A. Preston of Binghampton, N. Y., price 50c. A pamphlet of 74 pages, about the size of our largest poultry magazines. Devoted to the Wyandotte with other valuable information.

The Advertisers' Gazette, a monthly paper for advertisers, published by R. L. Watkins, Advertising Agent, Prospect. Ohio., 16 pages. price 50c. per year.

Farming on Green Manures, by Dr. Harlan. See his advertisement.

Progressive Housekeeping ; or keeding house without knowing how and knowing how to keep house well. By Catherine Owen, author of "Ten Dollars Enough." "Gentle Breadwinners." and " Molly Bishop's Family." 16mo, $1.00. Houghton. Mifflin & Co., Boston. In this book Mrs. Owen gives a series of chapters on the art and method of keeping house well, full of practical sense tested by experience.

TO BOOK PUBLISHERS.

Books received during the season will be taken notice of and acknowledged in the next issue of the Manual, if they are of such a character that I can permit my readers to know of them through this publication.

Magazines and pamphlets will also be noticed under this heading.

"Pine Tree State Seed" Still takes the lead.

TRASH SEEDS · CHEAP SEEDS · STORE SEEDS · OLD SEED · GOOD SEED · BETTER SEEDS · SEEDS (Pine Tree State)

6 KINDS OF CHOICE POTATOES FREE to every customer. Write for my Catalogue of *best* Vegetable and Flower Seeds, and read all about this unparalleled offer. Also about the new FILLBASKET Potato. The ladies will be interested in my $10 PANSY PRIZE. Address, mentioning Howe's Potato Manual, **W. H. EASTMAN, SEEDSMAN, EAST SUMNER, ME.**

USE BARKERS NERVE & BONE LINIMENT

BARKER'S HORSE, CATTLE & POULTRY POWDER

BARKER'S NERVE & BONE LINIMENT

PARIS GREEN

NOTHING BETTER FOR STOCK.—Mr. W. H. Metzgar, Merchant of Irvineton, Pa., in an order for Barker's Horse, Cattle and Poultry Powder says: "They excel all others. Nothing better for stock. It will recommend itself."

ADAM FOREPAUGH, the great showman and owner of 465 valuable horses, uses Barker's Horse, Cattle and Poultry Powder. A man with his years of experience, and owner of so many valuable horses is certainly worthy of example.

CHICKEN CHOLERA.—William A. Black of Jacobstown, N. J., in a correspondence, says: "I had heard of Barker's Horse, Cattle and Poultry Powder. I had cholera very bad among our Poultry, I used the powder for it and found it to be reliable."

BARKER, MOORE & MEIN,

No. 609 Market St., PHILADELPHIA, PA.

SUGGESTIONS.

All cultivating and hocing should cease as soon as the small potatoes begin to set, as great damage is done by distrubing the roots after that. The weeds should be under such thorough subjection before this time that the brai ching tops which now begin to cover the ground will prevent any further weed growth.

Good potatoes should contain about 25 per cent. of dry matter, which leaves three-fourths of their bulk for water.

Dig when the skin will not rub off under reasonable pressure with the fingers.

Lots of troub.e will be saved by killing the old beetles early in the season, which can be done by soaking some potatoes in strong paris green water or rolling pared potatoes in pure paris green and distributing along between rows.

After potatoes are dug put a half pint of air-slacked lime to a barrel of potatoes, which lessens the tendency to rot.

Where potatoes are cut they should be allowed to dry a day or two which prevents the tendency to rot after planting, especially if rainy weather sets in.

Small potatoes are used with excellent results by an extensive poultry establishment near Amherst to take the place of an equal bulk of ground grain in a feed composed of two-thirds boiled potatoes and one-third ground grain.

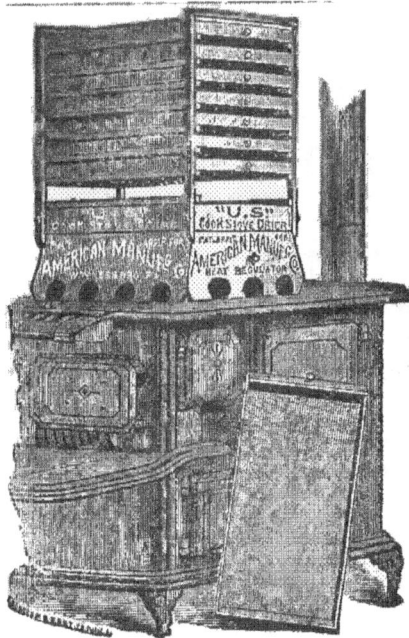

I believe the Fruit Evaporator illustrated at the left is of such value to every farmer that I offer it to my patrons at a grert bargain.

Price, delivered at cars at the factory, $7.00. I will give $2.00 worth of potatoes from my list with one of these dryers for $7.00. You cannot buy one at the factory for less than $7.00. If you should want one in the summer after it is too late to get potatoes, write to me, and if not too great I will pay freight charges as an inducement to purchase through me.

MISCELLANEOUS SEEDS.

I will supply you with seeds in *packets* from any seedman's catalogue of the country at a discount of 20 per cent. from their list. At
that rate 5 cent packets would be 4 cts. and 10 cent packets 8 cts.,
and a dollars worth of packets 80 cts. No order accepted at this
rate for less than 20 cents worth nor later than March 20. I make
this proposition to accommodate my customers who may want only a
few packets of some seedman's seeds, and might not get them other-
wise. It will save you a little trouble and expense. I shall be in
constant receipt of goods from the many seed growers and dealers
during the season and give you the advantage of my wholesale rates
without charge.

In ordering under this proposition, state name or number of what
you want with the list price and the full address of the one who ad-
vertises it.

In many instances under this offer I shall lose money but on the
average expect to clear myself.

If you want certain seeds and are not particular from which of the
many reliable houses they shall come, it will accommodate me by
giving me the option in the matter. as I might be sending an order
the day yours is received, and thus it would save me a little trouble.

THE FOLLOWING TABLE is offered for study, to those who wish
to compare the relative productiveness of different varieties of potatoes. Of the two varieties on page 71 marked with * the weights
were not given. The Early Rose is also number 15 under the 20
column by duplicate planting. Vick's Extra Early in the 133 column is also number 117 for same reason. In the first test (116 column) there were four duplicate plantings. This calculation is made
up from the first, where the seed used was saved from the largest
tubers of the most productive hills of the year previous.

Until the last thing before going to press I expected to add another
column giving the result of my own test of most of the varieties. I
decided not to give it this year and that explains why a few names
are given with no figures opposite. Look out for this list next year
with those also of several other tests not given in this table. In any
one of the tests the varieties marked 1 out-yielded the others and
they are marked accordingly to the poorest yielder. Many cases
occur where two or more varieties yielded the same. In such cases
the variety coming first alphabetically is given the highest place.

See special offers and premiums on potatoes, elsewhere, good till
March 20.

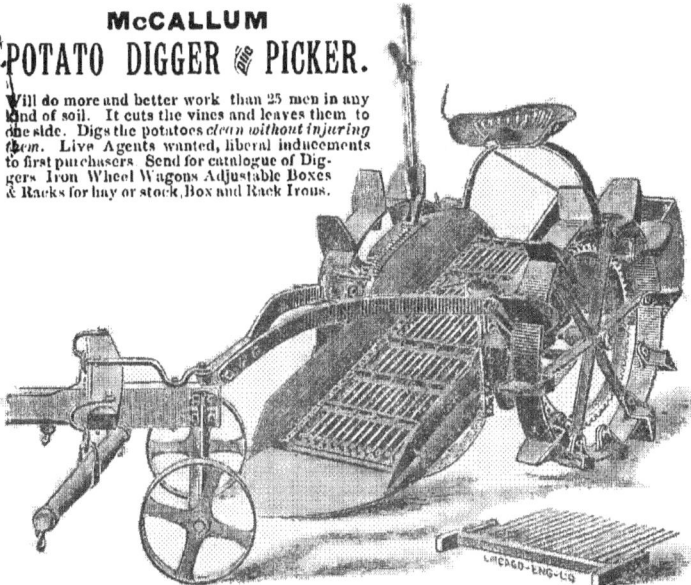

Stockbridge Potato Manure.

BONELESS PER ACRE.

FERTILIZER CO.,